RITUALS

Jenkins

ISBN: 978-1-915079-00-8

Cover design by Aaron Kent

Edited & Typeset by Aaron Kent

Broken Sleep Books (2022)

Broken Sleep Books Ltd
Rhydwen,
Talgarreg,
SA44 4HB
Wales

Contents

"I have done nothing; is there a God?"
— *Helen Duncan (1897 – 1956)*

-

Last person sentenced under the British Witchcraft act of 1735, part time factory worker, mother of six.

Rituals

E. P. Jenkins

Introduction
— Briony Hughes

It's the 2019 Small Publishers' Fair at Conway Hall, Bloomsbury. We are in 'The Green Room'. Seven mismatched chairs make a semi-circle. The space smells faintly of musk; this was expected.

I invite E.P Jenkins to the centre for her performance. She is wearing lace [irrelevant but a detail that I remember]. She sits and waits. A dress is draped across her lap – its material hangs over the arms of her chair.

It will occur to her that cowl sounds an awful lot like scowl
cast on 20

Jenkins begins to sew. Sheets of printed type are lifted toward the hem of the dress and then tacked on. I remember red thread – thick – though this may be a false memory. Each stitch is meticulous, as is the precision of her voice. Her hand movements follow the rhythm of language, or perhaps language follows the pattern of her hand movements. There is a connection between Jenkins' hand and her voice that extends into the thread into the dress into the chair into the room into the air into the audience into me.

k2tog, k2, yo, k1, yo

In *Spontaneous Particulars: The Telepathy of Archives*, Susan Howe articulates, 'Words are skeins – meteors, mimetic spirit sparks.'[1] Howe's archival telepathy is materialised through the image of a bundle of yarn. Language becomes an object of craft, which can be threaded, tied, woven, knitted, spooled, and stretched, offering textual associations between temporal and geographical barriers. These points of convergence are fragmentary and wavering but allow the 'disparate strands' of archived objects to knot together, sparking in moments of mimesis and connection.[2]

Like Howe, Jenkins is interested in poetics-as-craft, and the possibilities that may emerge from this practice. Through *Rituals*, Jenkins offers the figure of the witch as a lyrical reimagining of Susan Howe's skein. Whilst the witch's crafting rituals [often quite literally] weave in and out of the human experience, language, domestic objects, and the natural world, the

---

1   Susan Howe, *Spontaneous Particulars: The Telepathy of Archives* (New York, New Directions Publishing, 2014) p. 26.
2   Johnathan Creasy, 'Susan Howe's Telepathy', *LA Review of Books* [online] <https://lareviewofbooks.org/article/susan-howes-telepathy/> [accessed 10/08/2021].

witch's body also extends fibres across boundaries – roots sprout from the tips of the witch's fingers, a rabbit kit grows between spinal vertebrates, shopping-list-mulch lines her pockets, 'the witch's garden is the witch'.

Jenkins' work moves on and off the page: performance rituals become text-based poems and text-based poems become rituals. Carefully and curiously her reader/audience/passer-by becomes intertwined with or knotted into the collection.

███████████████████████████ practice ████████████████████ ████
███ Witchcraft ████ practice ██████████ culturally
and societally, ███ thus ███ be difficult to define ████
████████████████████████████████ be ████████ with
caution.

The Witch's manifesto

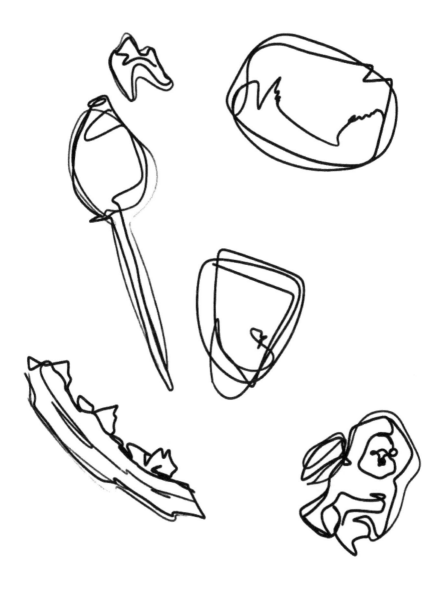

Defining

Rituals are

Gardening - part. 1

Plant hands into soil, remember, she must wait
for the hairs on her knuckles to grow.
This will take time, but they will grow.
Crystalline paper cuts and nicks from ant bites
 (ants may vary)
will be praised open from the inside by new,
fresh, raw fingers with bible page skin and
nothing to lose. From their tips roots will sprout.
And through them she
will drink.

Reading

The witch will talk to books when she picks them up address them by name say
     hello book
but with an *oo*
     like moo
say
     hello b*oo*k
they appreciate the roundness of the sound against their cracking spines

Childcare

It is irresponsible to ritualise childcare. Instead,
marvel at her flower bud hands. Watch
as they unfurl in an attempt to steal the witch's
last salt and vinegar crisp.

"difficult to define"

Dog Walk in the Woods or Jawbone

Premolar 308, 307, 305, canine 304 vulpes
vulpes pulvis et cinis pulvis et cinis canidae
carnivora.

Matriphagy - consumption of the mother by
her offspring
        is a jaw bone.

Parasitic wasps eat their way out of their
stepmothers.
        I'm sure that's not the same thing.
        I'm sure stepmothers would disagree.

A wet snout snuffles at a dry one. The dog
is interested in what I am doing because
        the dog is always interested in what I
am doing.

Restless fox agitated by the rabbit in their
teeth
        308 307
longs for a toothpick.
Just like the witch they'll shovel down dirt
always causing trouble I'll call you kitsune of
the Kentish Downs.   Vulpus invictas.

an archaeologist's plastic nails digging
graves to free the dead. A soiled caesarean
        section.

Matriphagy or bottle tops that nestle next to
dead teeth, jewels in a crown in coca cola.
E150apremolar 308E150bcanine 304.
Jawbone jutting out of the dirt glacier in a
sun-baked sea.

        You only get to see about 30% or so
        they say. Soon that'll be all that's left.

Skin care

Grind one juniper berry and a pearl of
mother's wisdom until dusty
                  skin on my knees and knuckles
flake like moths' wings.
5% lactation
         to be applied as liberally as
the witch   applies herself
      to a lick, split scrape
                  in the middle of her forehead.
Love the skin you're in   so much
you pull it off in strips.
                            Maypole yourself in ribbons.
            Suspended in an oil chrysalis,
marvel at your tender bleeding edges.

Hex via Scarf – a Magikal Knitting Pattern

It will occur to her that cowl sounds an awful lot like scowl
        cast on 20
if she could wrap a tight red line mouth around her neck instead this would all
go a lot faster and she needn't keep an eye on the mounting tension
        k2tog, k2, yo, k1, yo,
images of angry sheep, she will try not to laugh this is very serious work
        k2, sls 1, k1, passo
the texture of crunchy nylon wool makes some people's last never stand on
edge hers is perched on the end of the needle standing on its head
        p 20 on the wr side
of bed this morning, maybe that's why it all feels so crunchy
        rep row 1
but she never learns her lesson holding on to all this grief only makes
        rep row 2, cont…
cast off
        whip st two ends together in an infinite loop
the hex is sealed
        hand wash in cold water

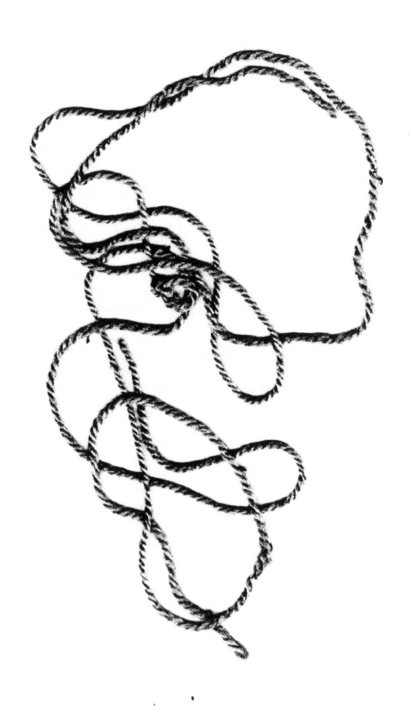

sticky with

ant   ants   ants   ants   ants   ants

Descaling

Hassle free   cheap
an overnight lemon cut into
the cliffs of Dover

here the water is
        hardly worth your time
Vera Lynn.

        humming while it
hums it
hums
it
        did you
unplug it first?

Enough to write your name on a blackboard
thick and viscus cleaning
        compact or
flaking.

Definitely flaking. Soft
crumbling hum. Witches hum for their tea with
        a squeeze of lemon and
vinegar solution.

Where is the plastic
            filament
the plastic doodad   ?
        We'll meet again.

Spell via Laura's Biscuits

- Take one cup of just enough
- A teaspoon
- Three pinches of happy birthday
- Enough milk to create islands

Disintegrating moth wing page dust. Sit and listen. Still. Listen. Scrape. Scraping. Bone clunks against wood. Dry bones. Desert bones. Dessert bones.

Turgid lumps. Big enough to make a splash. Don't. Lay still. Motion absorbed by the universe's packing material. Wait. Tucked away into quiet caverns. Oscillating stillness.

There is softness to the scraping. Listen. In one ear a hand gropes for something tangible. Falls through like time. Like ants. Scraping. Scuttles up. Like rain at sea.

Valley dwellers all drown. If there were any. Listening. The witch would have been sad. Or paused. At the stop sign spoon with half its head cut off.

Bread

Gnawing, gnashing,   fork prongs
otherwise known as
            glass jaw
     tines.
5 letters 4 down

clench

grind like millstones into
       antibiotics may affect an

aching ear
      despair grows
up from the ground like wheat.
Beats like a drum. Drum

wheat is the best kind for making
      no it

doesn't grow here.

A scythe because people are like
pasta   but
I'll make bread.

Prove it, in a
 warm dark place where
         hedgehogs like to burrow so always

grow and rise and

check your bonfires before setting them alight

      heat

claws up her legs
      is this normally

what it looks like before its topped with an egg and

      antibiotics and twigs

darkens, hardens, the surface

      of Mars was once
of the crust.

Slice it and toast it, in a
                two in one
body of water similar to

jam
thick
      dosage may
hide the taste.

elongated

tangled

en tan gled

Migraine or A Rabbit

There is a rabbit growing in the rift between two vertebrates of the witch's spine

it tests its new muscles by shakily flexing little legs wrapped in oiled fur wettened by spinal fluid it floats in amnionically

C3 and C4 roll and crack while small paws look blindly for more room awkwardly shifting cartilage and sloshing the witch into sea sickness

    make a burrow in her muscle chasms sweet rabbit

says the witch to her passenger

    but, please. Sit. Still. Listening.

The desired effect of valerian root dried and ground

    wet, sweet, and cold she will lay face down in the back garden and encourage the dirt to fill her eyes

freeing schools of birds that fly from the cracks behind her ears which the soil could not plug

scared away by the rabbit's growing anger

quelled a little by the scrape, scrape, scraping of rough porcelain against willow bark

the crone told the witch that its daughter is aspirin

but that will never numb her to the look of pink flesh of tree under screwdriver.

Cauterising a wound

The witch's mark is
iodine coloured.   A stain.
Under our left breast
          denotes where

Sebastian's subtle arrow hovers over send
snapped at the hilt
                    left to rot
embedded on the ocean floor a sunken ship

no amount of washing
will remove the smell. The devil is indelible
          ink. Burn. Burning
chemicals
          in the nostrils that
erodes her brain like
sea-side cliffs like
          coastal drift like
           acid

rusting
          flaky when it is exposed for too long
no course of action to take at this point

precious metals were much sought after in
          our etched memory.
                    Scar tissue
purple. Was the first sign that

rot has taken hold.

The plaster he slapped on
over the sore
          will not
          did not stop.
Stop

How it festers.

Putrefied, was the state in which they found the
        fig cleaved open
        emits
sweet smell of decay recognisable to all who

intolerable to none and she

work closely with the dead.

Bulging buboes
    that should be lanced
        a knight and his weapon of choice in most court festivities.

No amount of dried herbs and smoke can stop
contamination through osmosis

        revolt

 bind it with clean gauze
and wait
wait
        it will devour us whole

there is no balm or salve to apply
no chalky pill or rose or mercury
        to choke down
incision
        exorcise
the tumour

it is time
        metastasize   cancer cannot be allowed to spread
cannot escape
        bloody fingers
    they search in the darkness

in the meantime
        hide
straddle her brain and
hide

pluck at an   optic nerve
it
is a ghost in the

                                        peripheries

a shadow on the future
but it   cannot hide indefinitely.
So,

a witch will rip our eyes out
if she has to.

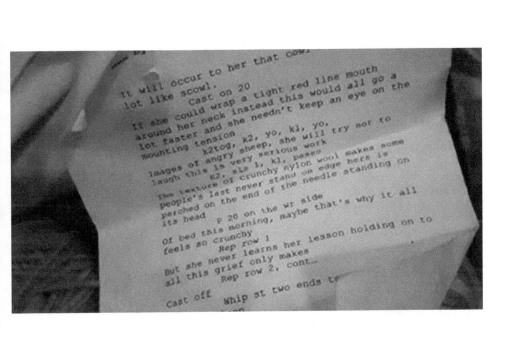

It will occur to her that cow
lot like scowl.
    Cast on 20
If she could wrap a tight red line mouth
around her neck instead this would all go a
lot faster and she needn't keep an eye on the
mounting tension
    k2tog, k2, yo, k1, yo,
Images of angry sheep, she will try not to
laugh this is very serious work
    k2, sl5 1, k1, psso
The texture of crunchy nylon wool makes some
people's last never stand on edge hers is
perched on the end of the needle standing on
its head
    P 20 on the wr side
Of bed this morning, maybe that's why it all
feels so crunchy
    Rep row 1
But she never learns her lesson holding on to
all this grief only makes
    Rep row 2, cont...

Cast off   Whip st two ends t

Divination

Divining for the witch's body
         of water
where is this still water
leeched with chalk and waste
no active intervention
her own Swordy Well
lays patiently impatient no current plans to build any defences
         at the bottom of
the dark pits   it sits
motionless and cold holding the existing defence line
quiet and cavernous   maintaining
aggressively stagnant
swarming with little
blood worms   managing realignment
         in
ghastly pirouettes
she   feels them inside
         advance the line
allowing the shoreline's agonising contortions.
The dyke within groans   moving to an agreed position
she had built it
         a new defence planned
to hide the swelling
waterline erosion   pressure burns and
starts restlessly extending the
         ground broken today
pierced the fleshy turf till its expanse reaches out beyond the designated
area out to
water springs   in full orbs
up, out of her eyes
filtered through   shoreline management
the silt of time
         will lead to further
flooding of the well

weavingweavingwavingweavingweavingweavingweavingweavinweavingweaving

New prescription

Drowsiness insomnia   fatigue

May flowers
vary and result in
       honey coated
sexual problems

please consult a physician if   lavender
       begins to grow
from the witch's eyes
       itching

headache tremor
drymouth
a sense of
              willow bark
       agitation

a natural source of

palpitations hoarseness
please
tremor
tremor
call

       dried and ground
nervous fatigue.

Agitation restlessness cloves and
       the inability to maintain
       ginger

consult   agitation
       raspberry leaf tea is
excessive

fatigue
excessive   pestle
muscle weakness dry mouth a sense of mint leaves

abnormal   salivation.

Breast pain weight gain
tension in the
          rosehips

do not take while
sexual problems   persisting

blocked nose
runny nose and nutmeg

intermittent constipation.
constipation blurred vision
and   camomile
mood   swings

very rarely but
               chili powder   finger tip stains
exhibited in some.
Consult   ataxia

- or,   the inability to control   st John's
muscle movements

very rarely   taken   raw ly
results can
          be taken orally

persistently
persistent
vomiting   of
          cured   petals.

beating

dusty

wi   ngs

Buying Second-hand Furniture

Wanted words we haven't said yet
written on
shopping lists
that the witch will find
mulched in her pocket
after a spin in the washing machine
words a strings of pearl
which she'll pull
on to speak
the words of others
that she has bought

Buying Second-hand Furniture part 2

For sale
one
slightly used
hour
just one
previous owner
an orange segment
thick with pith
plucked from a
fragrant pitted cradle
seeds that sprout
out of her mouth
mid-bite
full of promise
she can't
see yet
non-refundable

Recycling

Lost

      a sense of peace and contentment

          a sneeze

          an eyelash last seen on a nameless cheek

          a pair of sunglasses from Costa Rica
          dropped into the sea

          a mountain of plastic not
          lost but hidden from sight

          a scrap of carrier bag trapped
          in the throat of a sea bird

          a tiny piece of Barbie's head that ends
          up in the ovary of an emperor penguin

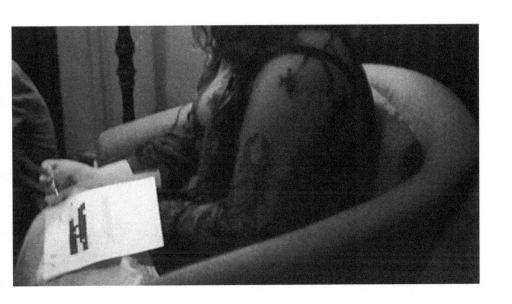

drenched in

h　　o　　n　　e　　y

like

ants ants ants ants weaving

Descaling part two

Ideal for the toughest   five minutes before
washing away
an essential service

1.6 – 2.5 litres
soap scum
        per day
these volumes are
watermarks   used regularly with
minimal impact on the environment   point 6

depending on
        water body
constitution   1.6 point
2
percent of daily fluid intake

for the sole purpose of hot, damaged, or acid sensitive
sugar free minimisation   500
       for several minutes

scrubbing and   metabolic oxidation can
remove contact lenses
do not breath annually to   guarantee the best possible
household bleach

20 – 40
point
      6   point
1
percent pints
2.5 point 2   point 1   point
500 ml of
sugar sweetened drinks

if present   limescale
no.1
point
2.5
          point
treatment plan

WHO continues rinsing
          with   benzyl salicylate
drinking water   maximum 0
point
0.5

hygienic conditions
promote
          skin irritation
point 0
perfectly safe

water supply networks
          in the kitchen and in
the eyes   are underground
2.5   meters
respectfully
6 percent

namely surface water such as
enamel, natural stone or skin
accounts for 68   point
4 point   percent
will cost around a penny.

Bird Watching

```
                                        e are, no
                                        e of, no
                                      ers, yellow,
                                    ike a jagged
                                     , is a shot

                               ldfinch
                             e of a child
                             ss the roof ki
                            aspberry jam
                            bles which I wi
                            You are sticky a
                          , tick breeze
                           impermanent card
                      y eye lids for win
                                        Two wings
                   , are           Hot air
              tune of, not gold,
          like own jagged Morris    from the
                              yellow       Ribbon
            white, is a shock to
                                        You
          a goldfinch            You
       acros                  ckib
    ny pe
```

Under

Gold leaf

The witch of late has been
       learning how to
guild things

                                                     gold

flakes crisp and fine metal skin

it's actually not that hard to
coat things in the fine
delicate facade
of an old high street bank
       sticky

paintings and notebooks
phones and wooden spoons
they too can shine like
          a light bulb   covered

unknowing gleam in the
       fog on the hillside in the wee hours

witches take fiddly metal
bees   wings
carefully though because
it can
stick
affix
to our fingertips

embed itself in the ridges of
       the chalky cliffs prime for erosion
with Maidus hands the witch

haloed
       breasts   like
twin saints
creases of
       the water ran divots in the riverbed's

          tights
next
immortalise   in   stone
impish hands
just backs
smooth soft ravines   of the river Stour
stirs the silt

this iridescent cover will protect the witch's skin from
her own restless clawing

watch the light
catch
the valleys of her   South Downs extend from
veins and tendons to
          cigarettes

the witch will try to catch
               tadpoles in   jam jars
with
her own light
against the wind

lastly
the witch will hold
          rabbit body
stomach that
has ached and hungered

cramped
doubled over with
          the lid affixed just so the
anxiety   can get in

the golden
          shoreline doesn't take too kindly to
manipulation

                                                              cracking

          which crawl across the surface
flakes
flutter into the breeze

witches
 have a habit of tarnishing

                                                     in saltwater

our shining exteriors
exposing the yolk inside
a bone thin   shell

dip us all
into   shining golden
       Saline solution
from time to time
to remind us   how

dishcloth

prayers

drenched in

a

'Hobgoblin' Advert

'Strong ales drawn from the cask'

Draw the witch from the casket
to drown her in the cask.
       A misidentified ducking stool misspelt
fucking
       it was installed by the landlord in 1962

cast her to the barrel
       a nunnery
with the hobgoblins
the witch will be dressed in
garlands of hops.

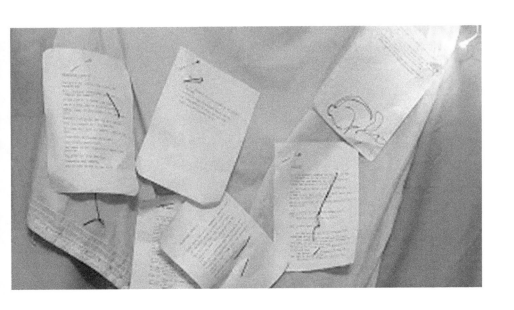

The Witch's Fluxus Score

Step one
Sit on the ground. Identify with the lettuce. If the witch cannot find lettuce, imagine a lettuce.

Step two
Be in the ground. Admire leaves. The witch is waxy and full of water. Crunchy. Slightly sweet. A little peppery.

Step three
The witch allows herself to rot.

Lettuce via Witch's Fluxus Score

Fog rolls across
the witch's green lake   arms
as bass   wave
disturbing the silt with
flickering shimmering   hands
                         tails
emerald leaves   fleshy
crunch full of   water
hang and sway waxily
watching
        friends succumb
to the passing of the summer
crisp and   soil   warmed
taken
by the wind
        sit on the surface
            in
of the lake's   skin like boats
sailing
into early morning haze

J U I C E

from

a

Family reunion

Brother of the witch   he is   a
shining glass receptacle,
tanks in human   form
half full to   the middle
of the road a cat with patches of
          water
swilling around   it
dripping and leaking   fur
potential of a childhood
          swallowed by the gulp-full
          drain
draining
unprepared, as we   are for the
heat of the sun
          bulb
bulbous
dries
what little water's left
          he is   the fish in
          river
tank
brace ourselves,
against   unnatural waves
walls
          gasping for air
by the   gulp-full
all the while
          drowning
                    in it

Gardening - part.2

The Witch, who has no time to wait for germination
will, instead, shovel down dirt with a teaspoon and remark
at how little it tastes like treacle.

She will know she is nearly finished when
aphids start to accumulate on her eyelashes, but,
She will not worry, her cat eats aphids.

Once her stomach is bin bag full
her womb will take the excess - this is the goal.
Vines grow up through veins and
curl around capillaries.

The cysts on her ovaries will burst like overripe
pea pods and from them pour
chamomile and foxglove.

The witch's garden is the witch.

chrysalis   popped

open

Acknowledgements

Gratitude to the hosts and organisers Small Press Book Fair 2019, Poetry Society Café, and David Dykes and Bethany Goodwill of *Big Trouble* for hosting events where *Rituals* began to take form.

A special thank you to Royal Holloway and the Poetic Research Centre, especially Redell Olsen and my poetic practice course mates; Briony Hughes, Laura Hellon Cat Chong, Sophie Shepard, Martina Krajňáková, Tiffany Charrington, Chloë Proctor, Tese Uhomoibhi, Tanicia Pratt, and Ariana Benson. As well as all the amazing and talented people I met through the course. All of whom I am proud to call peers and friends.

Thank you, Aaron Kent and the wonderful people at Broken Sleep Books for their hard work and support.

Lastly, a very big and special thank you to my amazingly supportive fiancé Miguel and my mum Jane, who inspired my love of reading and all things weird and wonderful.

LAY OUT YOUR UNREST

Lightning Source UK Ltd.
Milton Keynes UK
UKHW020740270322
400665UK00003B/7